Dearest Creature

Dearest Creature

Amy Gerstler

Penguin Poets

PENGUIN BOOKS
Published by the Penguin Group
Penguin Group (USA) Inc., 375 Hudson Street, New York, New York 10014,
U.S.A. • Penguin Group (Canada), 90 Eglinton Avenue East, Suite 700, Toronto,
Ontario, Canada M4P 2Y3 (a division of Pearson Penguin Canada Inc.) •
Penguin Books Ltd, 80 Strand, London WC2R 0RL, England • Penguin Ireland,
25 St Stephen's Green, Dublin 2, Ireland (a division of Penguin Books Ltd) •
Penguin Group (Australia), 250 Camberwell Road, Camberwell, Victoria 3124,
Australia (a division of Pearson Australia Group Pty Ltd) • Penguin Books
India Pvt Ltd, 11 Community Centre, Panchsheel Park, New Delhi – 110 017,
India • Penguin Group (NZ), 67 Apollo Drive, Rosedale, North Shore 0632,
New Zealand (a division of Pearson New Zealand Ltd) • Penguin Books (South
Africa) (Pty) Ltd, 24 Sturdee Avenue, Rosebank, Johannesburg 2196, South Africa

Penguin Books Ltd, Registered Offices:
80 Strand, London WC2R 0RL, England

First published in Penguin Books 2009

10 9 8 7 6 5 4 3 2

Page ix constitutes an extension of this copyright page.

Cover art: *The Trophy Room*, by Marnie Weber, from the Dollhouse Series, 2002.
Collage on photograph. Courtesy of the artist and Patrick Painter Gallery.

LIBRARY OF CONGRESS CATALOGING IN PUBLICATION DATA
Gerstler, Amy.
    Dearest creature / Amy Gerstler.
        p. cm.—(Penguin poets)
    ISBN 978-0-14-311635-6
    I. Title.
    PS3557.E735D43   2009
    811'.54—dc22   2009019882

Printed in the United States of America
Set in Waldbaum MT
Designed by Elke Sigal
Cover designed by Maggie Payette

For Benjamin

Contents

I. Refugee

II. Creaturely

III. Maidenly

IV.   Elegy

Acknowledgments

The author gratefully acknowledges prior publication of some of the poems in this book in the following: *American Poetry Review*, The Best American Poetry blog (http://thebestamericanpoetry.typepad.com/), *Brooklyn Review*, *Burnside Review*, *CAB/NET*, *Coconut*, *Columbia Poetry Review*, *DMQ Review*, *Flight*, *Jacket*, *MiPOesias*, *No Tell Motel*, *Ocho*, and *TriQuarterly*.

Special thanks to:

Brighde Mullins, Brian Tucker, Paul Slovak, Marnie Weber, Mimi Gerstler, Dinah Lenney, Tom Clark, Bernard Cooper, and David Lehman.

Dearest Creature

I.

Refugee

For My Niece Sidney, Age Six

Did you know that boiling to death
was once a common punishment
in England and parts of Europe?
It's true. In 1542 Margaret Davy,
a servant, was boiled for poisoning
her employer. So says the encyclopedia.
That's the way I like to start my day:
drinking hot black coffee and reading
the 1910 *Encyclopædia Britannica*.
Its pages are tissue thin and the covers
rub off on your hands in dirt-colored
crumbs (the kind a rubber eraser
makes), but the prose voice is all knowing
and incurably sure of itself. My 1956
World Book runs to 18 volumes and has red
pebbly covers. It begins at "aardvark"
and ends with "zygote." I used to believe
you could learn everything you'd ever
need by reading encyclopedias. Who
was E. B. Browning? How many Buddhists
in Burma? What is Byzantine art? Where
do bluebells grow? These days, I own five
sets of encyclopedias from various
eras. None of them ever breathed
a word about the fact that this humming,
aromatic, acid-flashback, pungent, tingly

fingered world is acted out differently
for each one of us by the puppet theater
of our senses. Some of us grow up doing
credible impressions of model citizens
(though sooner or later hairline
cracks appear in our façades). The rest
get dubbed eccentrics, unnerved and undone
by other people's company, for which we
nevertheless pine. Curses, outbursts,
and distracting chants simmer all day
long in the Crock-Pots of our heads.
Encyclopedias contain no helpful entries
on conducting life's business while the ruckus
in your skull keeps competing for your
attention; or on the tyranny of the word
"normal"—its merciless sway over those
of us bedeviled and obsessed,
hopeless at school dances, repelled by
mothers' suffocating hugs, yet entranced
by foul-smelling chemistry experiments,
or eager to pass sleepless nights seeking
rhymes for "misspent" and "grimace."
Dear girl, your jolly blond one-year-old
brother, who adults adore, fits into
the happy category of souls mostly at home
in the world. He tosses a fully clothed doll

into the inflatable wading pool in your
backyard (*splash!*) and laughs maniacally
at his own comic genius. You sit alone,
twenty feet from everyone else, on a stone
bench under a commodious oak, reading aloud,
gripping your book like the steering wheel
of a race car you're learning to drive.
Complaints about you are already filtering
in. You're not big on eye contact or smiling.
You prefer to play by yourself. You pitch fits.
Last week you refused to cut out and paste
paper shapes with the rest of the kids.
You told the kindergarten teacher you were
going to howl like a wolf instead, which you did
till they hauled you off to the principal's
office. Ah, the undomesticated smell
of open rebellion! Your troublesome legacy,
and maybe part of your charm, is to shine
too hotly and brightly at times, to be lost
in a maze of sensations, to have
trouble switching gears, to be socially
clueless, to love books as living things,
and therefore to be much alone. If you like,
when I die, I'll leave you my encyclopedias.
They're wonderful company. Watching you
read aloud in your father's garden, as if

declaiming a sermon for hedges, I recall
reading about Martin Luther this morning.
A religious reformer born in 1483, he nailed
his grievances, all 95 of them, to a German
church door. Fiery, impossible, untamable
girl, I bet you too will post your grievances
in a prominent place someday. Anyway,
back to boiling. The encyclopedia says
the worst offenders were "boiled without
benefit of clergy," which I guess means
they were denied the right to speak
to a priest before being lowered into scalding
water and cooked like beets. Martin Luther
believed we human beings contain the "inpoured
grace of God," as though grace were lemonade,
and we are tumblers brimful of it. Is grace
what we hold in without spilling a drop,
or is it an outflooding, a gush of messy,
befuddling loves? The encyclopedia never
explains *why* Margaret Davy poisoned her employer,
what harm he might have done her or whether
she dripped the fatal liquid on his pudding or sloshed
it into his sherry. Grievances and disagreements:
can they lead the way to grace? If our thoughts
and feelings were soup or stew, would they taste
of bile when we're defeated and be flavored

faintly with grace on better days? I await the time
and place when you can tell me, little butter pear,
screeching monkey mind, wolf cub, curious furrow-
browed mammal, what you think of all this.
Till then, your bookish old aunt sends you this missive,
a fumbling word of encouragement, a cockeyed letter
of welcome to the hallowed ranks of the nerds,
nailed up nowhere, and never sent, this written *kiss*.

Dearest Creature,

If I end up an arid isle of desirelessness,
it will be 1,000% your fault. Why don't you
write? Why make me beg? Are you even
reading these letters? Weren't we happy,
each in our own peculiar way, traversing
that rumpled no-man's-land, the Gobi desert
of our bed? Night of Too Many Body Fluids,
can we laugh about that now? And that tussle
in the motel tub when I accidentally knocked
you unconscious? A minor concussion.
Surely you've forgiven me. It's been
several decades. I was loving you so much
this morning, while brushing my teeth
and doing my hair. Remember that
abandoned car we found while hiking
in the middle of nowhere, tufts of grass
sprouting from the radio, gymnastic
acts we performed in its rusted-out chassis?
I'm just trying to depress you. (*Hah!*) How
am I doing? If you don't send me a letter soon,
I'll have to resort to forgery. Your white violets
have prospered and spread. Do you mind if I
go on a while longer? I have so many thoughts
zipping around my head and I'm trying to fit
them all into words that will win you back
and that's why my handwriting rushes

and floods, which is also true of my speech,
chatter that's been known to reach
unintelligible and perhaps irritating-
to-most-people speeds, though I always secretly
believed what I said and meant completely,
sweetly intelligible to you, even when the idea-
content was, well, a bit melted, or had been run
    through,
as you liked to quip, one of my several mental
blenders. Remember when you said, after we'd
camped near Crater Lake for a week,
that I looked like the sort of tree one sees
in a dream? I made fun of you all day. Called
you loony. But now, with your tangerine tree,
the one you planted and fed fireplace ash
all its first winter, covered with hummingbirds,
I know exactly what you were trying
to say that precious day. Dearheart: a single
word would be enough to summon me. All else
burns off like fog. I lie *vividly* awake. Waiting.

Sonnet

The small stone towers pictured on the other side of this postcard
are called Lanterns of the Dead. Lights are displayed at night in
    those tiny
portholelike openings at the top, to indicate the location of cemeteries
so penitents hiking through graveyards by torchlight (a popular
activity here, the allure of which is a complete mystery to me)
can find their way. The lace pillow slips in this hotel look as if
they're crocheted from loops of white icing. This creates the sensation
that one is sleeping with one's head on a large rectangular pastry.
The hotel manager, a man with a drooping mustache, greets his
squirmy young dog each morning, cooing, "Hello, Mr. Wiggling
    Gentleman."
Of course this sounds ever so much better in French. That's all for
    now, dear.
Kiss the baby for me. I trust his custardy little mind remains sweetly
unencumbered by thought. Determined as I am to return from this
    mission
in one piece, I see now why your daily prayers are soooo important.

Luncheon with the Etruscans

As reedbirds with mustard were served,
the youngest Etruscan proposed a toast.
"You who drink wine by the bowlful,"
he began, "you who loll and sprawl
on soft couches: even *your* minds
are not beyond decipherment." We
all raised our glasses and laughed.
Turns out citizens in this florid but
short-lived civilization believed all is
sacred, sentient, trembling all over,
just like us. Next course: broiled
plover on toast. Talk drifted
to the archaeological record,
"beyond this world" contexts, and how
many words our languages had for being
drunk. We exchanged gifts and bribes.
Breast of partridge larded and fried
came next. One of the loveliest gifts
we received was an ornate fired-clay
drinking vessel. The figures on it seem
to be dancing, though they might be
peering into a cauldron of fresh entrails,
trying to divine the future, or making
primitive pie filling. Etruscan cemeteries
were larger and more elaborate than
their villages for the living. That

shocked some members of our party
a bit. "But our sphinxes had wings,"
the Etruscan host bragged, as his
countrymen looked away. "Same for
our horses. Our satyrs had long dirty
fingernails, out to here," and he
measured one hand a good ten inches
in front of the other. Just then the room
went pungent with wild oregano and fennel.
"The smell of our backyards," one said,
and the youngest wept. When the cover
was raised from its dish, we gave their
braised quail with bacon a standing ovation.

Letter from the Middle Ages

The barbarians are colorful and inventive
and we envy the heck out of them. Six lashes
for monks who sing out of tune. Altar boys

get slapped for stuttering or coughing. My
youngest daughter, kidnapped after morning
Mass, energetically fended off every rescuer.

However unworthy or out of date, I send you
the peppercorn of my affections, the pinkening
pomegranate of my regard, praying hard

for these greetings to embrace you across the named
ages that divide us (though we're mindful that
history never falls into such simplistic divisions).

Not a hopeful century I'm stuck in, full
of haggard cooks, ragged armies, and few
laws, scribbled by tallow candles' grimy light.

Unicorns sightings provide faint consolation.
Attempts to enforce celibacy in the priesthood
continue to fail. (More about that later . . .)

Future-dwelling pen pal: my own era repels me,
whereas other places, times, and climes beckon.
Is there not some way we can, by Christ's grace,

trade places? Even if only for a day? I have
striven to locate myself in spirit in other ages,
alas, to no avail. Only your letters and the love

of my dear (if runty) ones sustain me. How I long
to yank open a "fridge" and stare in, zip a zipper,
channel surf, sample antibiotics and a hundred

other coming attractions your missives describe.
Except for this pesky death stuff, we're all fine here,
coming to tardy consciousness of our wickedness

every day, seizing the property of our weaker
neighbors, watching peasants get arrested,
valuing the sweet and savory equally in our cuisine,

and even while pawning hymnals to get money for drink,
putting all confidence in God. Boldly we ride into war,
Bible quotations emblazoned on our helmets. The barbarians,

who get to wear all the eye makeup they like,
find us comic. A handsome lot, not one among them
is odious, vulgar, or sluttish. Their eyes shine

with sweet wonder. Their breath smells of cloves.
Like shy virgins they clap their hands over their mouths
when they laugh, hiding perfect teeth made of stained glass.

A Million Happy Endings

You see, casseroles can shout too. Everything can.
—*Pablo Picasso*

Seeking relief from the tidelike pull of dark thoughts, I took some household objects into my confidence. "O useful friends," I began. "What am I to do? Marooned and wounded, I'm in the midst of an extended stretch of celibacy. Each time the last man I dated and I got to the brink of sex, he'd go pale and whisper, 'Let's just cuddle.' My boss takes great delight in making me cry. The troop of toothless parolees next door opened a car repair shop in their driveway. It's busy from midnight to five in the morning, with jobs that require chain saws and rivet guns. Police helicopters swoop back and forth over my block all night, shining searchlights into bedroom windows. My brain is a smoldering train wreck, full of sinister information and . . ." The waffle iron yawned greasily. "It's your own damn fault. Why didn't you move to a better neighborhood when you could afford it? Oh, for Christ's sake don't cry. I was only joking." The faded tablecloth looked ashamed. Its fringe continued to fray. "Quit whining," rasped the cracked glass pitcher. She was feeling a bit choked, as I'd cut a bunch of begonias and jammed their stems into her open throat. I poured myself some club soda to settle my stomach. "Water's for sissies," the tumbler mumbled. "After all you've been through, what you need is vodka, pronto." The light of day mocked me. "A couple of slaps in the face, a few fresh setbacks, and suddenly you're numbering yourself among the slain? Give me a break." During a lull in the conversation, a hand-painted china plate explained, "You suffer the trials and transformations of middle age. Yes, there are annoyances and betrayals. Yes, loves fall away. That doesn't mean you give in." For several minutes an atmosphere of gravity and forgiveness seemed to prevail in the kitchen. Pink and black peppercorns nattered happily in their grinder. "We who are about to be pulverized salute you!" Down the long hall, the bed was remarkably welcoming. "Come to me," it whispered. "Climb aboard and drift for a spell. We'll find some windswept piney islands, and you can go ashore and colonize them if you like." I thought about the soul's wilderness, still unexplored at this late date. So began an unmapped and provisionless voyage. I threw my clothes overboard and watched them sink. Immediately I felt lighter, like a woman whose health has been recently restored. Peering over the edge of my barge, I could see a beautifully appointed ballroom at the bottom of the deep water, complete with coat-check rooms, mirrored walls, and lounges carpeted in a bold pattern of red and yellow quarter moons. There were rows of round tables, with candles aglow on each, and beyond that an oblong mahogany dance floor. People were dancing the Lindy, the shimmy, and the mambo. The bandstand was lit with colored spotlights as though a show was about to begin. Can you fathom the serene feeling it gives to float over a drowned ballroom? And now everything slows way down. We must wait patiently to see who steps out onstage to entertain us, to warble and croon, struggling to attain his or her perfect form, clad perhaps in dark green sharkskin or a silvery gown encrusted with pearls.

Moon Salutation

Even as I sleep in a ravine
on a mattress of dead grass,

bright jawbreaker,
I do salute you.

Don't look askance as my
stomach rumbles, ravishing

omelet, buttermilk layer
cake, bubbling four-cheese

pizza. O washed-out mandala,
radiant, featureless, cratery

face afloat in a bowl
of 4,000-year-old noodles:

don't let me be dimmed
by injury. Drape me in your

knowing corona. Let me sip
the skeleton tea you're steeping.

Keep our intimate religion top secret.
Even if it's only reflected light,

let me shine a while longer.

II.

Creaturely

Advice from a Caterpillar

Chew your way into a new world.
Munch leaves. Molt. Rest. Molt
again. Self-reinvention is *everything*.
Spin many nests. Cultivate stinging
bristles. Don't get sentimental
about your discarded skins. Grow
quickly. Develop a yen for nettles.
Alternate crumpling and climbing. Rely
on your antennae. Sequester poisons
in your body for use at a later date.
When threatened, emit foul odors
in self-defense. Behave cryptically
to confuse predators: change colors, spit,
or feign death. If all else fails, taste terrible.

Moths

lapel pins
for widow
or widower

eyes like
tiny burn
holes

hair ornaments
for ailing maidens

the house is full of them
between seasons:
brown scraps
of singed tissue
on which cryptic laws
are written

they fly awkwardly
as if nursing
old injuries
or rising
from bonfires

many lack mouths
of those who *can* eat
some feed on wool
feathers, fur, hair
leather, dust, tidbits
of linen: a vacuum
cleaner's diet
what kind of appetite
do they bring to pink
sweaters?

one drops
into your lap,
tiny dry dirt-colored leaf
whirring,
or it lights on your
sleeve
and you gasp

is it bad luck
when they land on you
these grubby
bits of missives
from limbo?
lint from God's pockets?
God's tapped off
cigarette ash?

dead they are majestic
toasted flowers,
nature's punctuation

just like us,
orchards spring
from their corpses

He

He wonders why there are no tigers in the Bible.
He thinks someone should consider putting them in.
He can be the very soul of elation. Yet some days
he's too sad to even button his coat. An impetuous man,
not entirely bound by natural laws, he never gets enough
kissing or figures out what kind of animal he is.
An impoverished doctor or handsome drifter,
when he sees a woman carrying a sick child wrapped
in an old plaid coat into the emergency room
he rushes over to help her. No coward soul is his,
though he is given to copious groaning. He once
wrote a play called *Eight People Who Are Really
Tired.* The audience loved it. When he and his brother
were thirteen and fourteen, respectively, they took LSD
in a tree house their father had built. For seven hours
he watched his cells vibrate wildly in time with cells
in the tree's trunk and leaves. Now, thirty years later,
he's never entirely forgotten that feeling.
It's been raining for days. He seems content
to stand on the covered front porch, under the dripping
eaves, smoking and petting his adoring sheepdog.
Whenever it rains like this, he remembers the one offense
his dad spanked him for when he was a kid.
He knows he deserved it. He sits down on the welcome
mat, taps off his ash, and kisses the dog's furry head.
She wiggles her hindquarters and licks the knee of his jeans.

In gleaming moments like these, forming and falling
like raindrops, I'd give anything to be one of them,
either that man or his dog. Instead, not knowing
which end is up, or what saints to pray to,
I find myself hopelessly in love with them both.

Chanson

Seriously undermedicated, I waltz
downstairs into the soaked street
during a short storm. No one but
the new dog home to advise against
it, and he decides to come along.
Rain pelts us like pills spilling from
the pharmacist's pockets as she does
a quick headstand to clear her mind
before another trying lunch with her
mother. The wet dog shakes himself
hard, license tags jingling like dimes
in a jar—a sound halfway between
maracas and breaking glass. I must
waltz carefully across sidewalks alive
with promenading snails, defenseless
and jellyish. Their motto: the wetter
the better. The dog licks a snail once,
unpersuaded by its flavor. I'm ruining
my boiled-wool bedroom slippers
in multiple puddles. You loved puddles
and tide pools, dear friend. Now
you are dead and I'm left not high
enough and not dry, wavering
in the rain, only snails and a spotted
dog urinating on geraniums for company.
I'd better not wander far in this drugged

weather, with the primitive cinema
in my head showing old cartoons
of pent-up rapture and despair,
and the sky gone violet, and everybody's
rain gutters continually drooling.

Birds of America

Naked and truthful, the birds of America
joined forces under a pale winter sun
that hung over my house like a sucked
cough lozenge or spooked moon
for what felt like centuries but in truth
was just the season of my comeuppance.
Black-and-white warblers, house wrens,
fox sparrows, and finches built intricate
yet causally tousled nests resembling
scarecrows' hairdos, right out in the open,
where I could easily see them, and nuthatches
too, but I was quite blind. Briefly seen,
though not by me, was the sickly
heroin bird who nods off midtwitter,
waking in late spring craving Kool-Aid
and Halloween candy. Vireos appeared—
not much to look at yet armed with warm,
winning personalities if you but trouble
to get to know them. Nature thus
seductively rustling her petticoats
could not touch me for the longest time
after you left. I was deaf to the eerie orchestra
of crickets *seep- seep- seeping* on tepid
summer eves and did not taste the pot
brownies friends offered, which I dutifully
chewed but could not get me high.

Nor did expertly mixed gin and tonics
flecked with colorless pulp of fresh lime
take the edge off, enliven me, or give me
peace. Nor could pork chops fried
with apple slices rouse me, nor the smell
of potatoes lyonnaise, nor did the clownish
antics of a handsome black Labrador
cavorting by the frilly hem of the foaming ocean
make me grateful. Then fall hurled itself down
with its customary thud. Intrepid birds
of America, you persisted though I was
such a goner. Scruffy starlings—not considered
desirable birds but dear to me now, modest
thrushes and buntings, and male quail
with topknots like commas: there was no
flourish of trumpets or 21-gun salute heralding
the recovery of one who'd believed herself
dead, only more birdsong persevering till
I could finally hear again. Though I know full
well it was never your feathered intent to revive
me, still I find myself deeply in your debt. These
flung handfuls of millet, peanuts, and sunflower
seeds hardly seem a fitting or rich enough reward.

Interview with a Dog

Q: Why on earth did you eat that ten-dollar bill? It can't have tasted nice.

A: Don't be gruff. Anything that falls on the floor is mine. Can I have a cookie now to change my mouth lining flavor? Can I? Can I?

Q: What does it mean to be runt of the litter?

A: Stomped-on lowest rung. Everyday fear bath, nonstop bow down. Wreathed in terror reek that broadcasts you are last of the last. I don't like to talk about this stuff . . .

Q: OK. I just gave you a bath. Then you went and rolled in manure.

A: Will you barbeque soon? Will you let me lick the grill when it cools?

Q: No, really. How come I get you all nice and clean and you immediately roll in something stinky?

A: Humans don't get true grooming, which only takes place using the tongue. Toothpaste, mouthwash, and deodorant are what's "stinky." Soap's revolting. Terrible invention. Why have it in your lamplit, carpeted, door-locked lair? Dung is informative, complex—full of news flashes from the body's interior. Shit's an encyclopedia, volumes of urgent correspondence your organs wrote, if only you knew how to read. What's learned from smelling shampoo?

It just causes sneezing, erases articulate fumes. Bull-dozes olfactory signposts. Washing is book burning.

Q: How come you chew window blinds during thunder-storms?

A: Must break hard things with teeth—bite, crunch, tear when scared. Need escape hatch fast. Eat my way out.

Q: Well, that makes a certain sort of sense. But why did you roll in the carcass of that dead seal when we took you to the beach at Morro Bay?

A: To transfer ghost cloak of invisibility, silly. Death smell lends protection. Winner of ripest warm-day-decay contest is not challenged by pack peers—billowing pu-trefaction blasts inspire respect and great kill pride! Meat-rot bouquet is prey smell's best medal. What don't you understand that?

Q: Hmm. And what motivated you to eat that postcard from Alex and chew up several of my Catholic saint statuettes?

A: Doesn't make a lick of sense to me. THERE'S THE CAT! GET HIM! (*Races out of room.*)

Chant of the Hallucinogenic Plants

God made nothing in vain. All herbs have purpose.

Pollinated by bats (which tickles!) we ripen the mind.

Sip our bitter milk. Smoke these leaves and shepherd

the immense. This blossom, when swallowed,

makes cowards eloquent. Haze of consolation

robs grief of her sting. Everything drips and merges.

Phosphorescent radiations overtake you. The banal

becomes ecstatic. Everlastingness pours forth.

Wrapped in a flame-colored cloud, swaddled

in mirth and trembly tenderness toward earth,

one prefers not to stir from this cave. God

is a substance, a drug. These erotic shocks,

this blizzard of images, this ambiguous wink

is his. Man is only a weed in these regions.

III.

Maidenly

At the Back of a Closet, Two Dresses Converse

You're the overthrow of all my former opinions,
a black taffeta dress says, faintly exhaling
Chanel. *You smolder with hidden narratives,*
a pink sleeveless sheath reveals. *I share*
many of your nauseas and dreads, the black cocktail
dress observes. *How touching I find your undermuslin's*
rustle, the pink dress admits, surprised to find
she's speaking so freely. They listen
for a few minutes to the chink of flagstones
being laid on the back patio.

You're the only one here I want to dance with,
the black frock lets slip. *Fair ladies—*
a leather jacket begins, but the black dress
interrupts, *Hush!!!* (She's the more severe
and immoderate garment.) The jacket gets mad.
You lesbian thrift-store remnants! he thinks. The clatter
of a silverware drawer being yanked open is heard.
We live more intensely in this cloistered, mothball-scented
enclave, don't you agree? the older dress asks.
Yes, my darling! affirms her organza companion.

Let us say nothing of feuds brewing among tumbled
pumps at the bottom of the closet, of ravenous handbags
dangling from hooks, of the clogged steam iron
who scorches ruffles and melts buttons,

of indelible yellow perspiration stains. Let's keep
eavesdropping but do nothing to disrupt this budding
sympathy between two disused evening dresses, who,
by virtue of having been hung up with a buffer
of silk blouses between them, cannot touch
or generate even a spark of static electricity.

How to Wear Hats

A girl enters a restaurant breasts first,
wearing a lamb's wool beret.
If the man she's meeting is made irate
by her hat, this happens because
he gets jealous and feels competitive
with her whole wardrobe, including
her shoes. Nervous people end up
with frivolous, unflattering hats,
so relax, goddammit. A woman's
heart history is revealed by the sad
tilt at which her cloche or fedora
is worn. Sweat stains graph a man's
virility on his hatband. Never work
yourself up into a hat tantrum
(otherwise known as "blowing
your lid"), which leads straight to brain
fever. Do not buy babies dark-
colored hats, which besmirch pastel
thoughts. Keep your newborn's soft
skull warm, or his hair will never grow
in thicker than pinfeathers.

The Chamber of Maiden Thought

Must we be merciful, a sweating damsel asks,
to ruined suitors and tragic dads, as this music demands,
even if we can't abide their stonemason's hands?
Can you see the vile light emanating from my petticoat
through this thin dress? I have something to unbosom.
Are special events taking shape inside your nervous system,
too? No more homemade candy for me: too much
love was drizzled over those popcorn balls.

The boys construct their own squirt guns, capable
of amazing trajectories. They're pitching tents, building
one-person canoes. Any night now they'll light out
for parts unknown. Then we'll be left to fend
for ourselves. Armed with only our silly dread
of night air, fresh-baked macaroons, and amateurs'
panic, we'll spend weeks trying to read their empty beds—
divining meaning from mussed sheets like tea leaves.

We smoke opium on wooden bunks in their abandoned
barracks, out behind the old greenhouse—a mosaic
of broken windows—leaking grievance without speaking,
forsaking our bodies, which lie on chintz bedspreads
like dropped opera gloves. Needing to be heard above the din,
wearing perfectly attentive breasts, we are easily comforted.
The pipes are big as oboes, so the music enters us gently,
again and again, till it's time to go home and poach salmon.

Female Deity

All names and forms begin in her.
Gouged out of solid rock, her tomb
looms near sacred aviaries where
her favorite birds of prey still nest.
Depicted naked with a capelike
mane of hair, she's the soil we've
sprung from, whose voracious
graves will digest us again
and again. Reputed to smell
virginal yet earthy—her scent
tinged with carnivorous whiffs of blood—
she's said to have borne twenty-odd
children, yet kept her figure boyish
and slim. The personification
of our fall, she is always near at hand:
when beseeching pleas receive
a slap, grunt, or shove for reply,
where fresh wounds go uncleaned
and true love has worn thin. Her voice
is heard in grave robbers' debates
about the rising prices of their wares.
Legend says a spurned lover
murdered her—cut her up
and heaved her limbless into the sea.
Her name means "eternal swimmer,
she who takes revenge when the enemy's

back is turned," though one young
scholar has translated it as, "goddess
most unerodable, who sprouts new
appendages endlessly and never truly dies."
All over the East one sees limestone
statues of her peacefully sleeping,
guarded by her little cat, Giblet,
baring his tiny stone fangs.

Always

Her name was Cloudveil. She claimed to have been raised
in a sunless, flowerless cave. Her handwriting was worse
than a nervous first grader's. While toweling off one night,
I caught her gulping my bathwater from cupped hands.
At first I thought, yuck! Then it struck me: this is love.
Mornings, she'd splash a little whiskey on her cornflakes.
She convinced me to swim in a chilly mountain lake, though
I hate both nature and being cold. "Come on! I've never had
a skinny-dipping regret," she said. The first symptom was
that she couldn't stop humming. After being awake five days
straight, she burned most of her clothes, sold her books
and stuffed animals. "I'm moved to amend my life and reinvent
my sorry mind." That's a quote. Before she left, she grabbed
my hands, kissed their grubby knuckles one by one. Wherever
she roams, may she sip from cosmic reservoirs. May cheering,
applause, oohs, and aahs (never boos, explosions, or groans)
be the sound effects in her head, come rain or come shine.

Untranslatable

He picked me up at a greasy spoon   made eyes at me
invited me back to his pad   where we smoked some rad
Acapulco gold in our birthday suits   cut to the next day
we split his crib   lit out for the nearest watering hole
knocked back a few zingers   and he starts giving me the
    third degree
whereupon I advised him to butt out pronto   he lights up a
    cancer stick
butter wouldn't melt in his mouth and get a load of this colossal
    nerve
he tried to put the bite on me right there in the speakeasy
for a hundred clams   like I would ever have that kind of dough
you can bet your sweet ass   I told him where to go
he said well don't have kittens about it and I hauled off and let
    him have it
right in the kisser   that's basically all she wrote   he wigged out
went ape busted up the place   the barkeep called the long arm
    of the law
and before you could say Jack Robinson they'd hauled
my new squeeze off to the hoosegow   damages will cost him
an arm and a leg when he gets out of the slammer
serves him right the two-faced galoot   the crumb   the no-
    good souse

keeping my eyes peeled I noticed a hunky Hercules in blue

he waved his nightstick at me   gave me the once-over

chatted me up   turns out he was on the level   got me all starry
    eyed

and weak in the knees   he's got two left feet sure but what a
    sweet

puss on him   it'll be a cold day in Hades before I take a powder

on this crew-cut Romeo, this dreamboat in uniform (he's square

as the day is long but his heart's in the right place) believe you
    me.

During a Wet Spring, Long Ago,

She became famous for her wit, her brains, and her ugliness.
Simple and frugal in her tastes, devout in thought
and manner of life, she married a former priest, who had
been freed from his vows, being unable to endure their rigor.
The cordials and elixirs habitually administered to him as a child
may well have developed the warring tastes for both stimulants
and opiates that almost ruined him. They were fanatically happy
for fifteen years, and when she passed on he wrote two lively,
amusing, and sensible texts on domestic harmony. His diary entry
for what was likely the first evening they spent alone together
consists of a single line: "We watched meteors the entire night."
His servants said that after her death he was seen to kiss her
picture every morning upon waking, every night upon retiring,
and at other times of day when he wrongly supposed he was alone.

Contrite

> Guilt only entitles the guilty.
> —*Robert Walser, "The Story of the Prodigal Son"*

Do excuse the luminous toxin that migrated
from the stash in my handbag to your tuna sushi.
Please accept my condolences on the fatal stabbing
(with a buttercream-encrusted cake cutter)
of the matron of honor at your wedding reception.
Forgive me for introducing your new husband
(the uprooted, sad-eyed Jew) to my stockbroker
as a "forlorn pork spurner." I meant no harm.
I just had nothing left in the tolerance tank.
For 8 weeks now I've been dating a grave robber
who'll never take me out at night. I'm sick
of lunches in broad daylight with this drowsy
guy who has lead-colored dirt packed under
his nails. Waiters stare at his hands like
they've seen a spook when he points out
what he wants on the menu, usually something
drowning in gravy. Most of all, pardon me
for riding roughshod over your tender confession
about poisoning your mother over the course
of a decade, a project you reported the results
of twice daily on your formerly anonymous
blog called Toxicmom.com.

Greece,
or
My Mother as Pola Negri

I.

In her eightieth year, having survived two wars,
three revolutions, and four husbands, my mother
announces we're sailing to Greece. Once again
I'm drafted as traveling companion.
"Think of it as a pilgrimage, darling," she cajoles
in that fake-sounding accent of hers.
Imperious, exotic, and still much sought after,
she was once a popular film star whose sly blend
of wit and innuendo confounded even the strictest
censors of her day. Born in Warsaw, she considers
herself "spiritually Greek." This has been the case
ever since her fourth husband, Mikos, died
in her arms on the dance floor decades ago.
Despite the fact that she cannot walk unaided
or hear much below a shout, she has booked us
on a three-week tour of Greece and its nearby islands. We
are to stay at the Hotel Cecil in the heart of old Athens,
with its magnificent roof garden and views of the Acropolis.
Her early years were spent in dire poverty. As soon
as she began to command lavish salaries, she devoutly
embraced excess. Stories are told of her ordering lychee
nuts flown to her film sets round the world—enough

for the entire cast and crew. Strong, passionate, earthy,
and still quite beautiful when she removes her glasses
(their lenses thick as storm windows), she'll mutter,
"That'll settle your hash," after indulging in some frisky
bit of wickedness. "I am but one infinitesimal mote
in the cosmos," she likes to sigh, rolling her eyes
heavenward. She's never above fainting to get her way.

II.

Here's a snapshot of me—the mousy, unmarried daughter—
juggling her hatboxes. That was the trip to Nepal, I believe.
Here's another of me bribing officials in Córdoba to allow
her rust-colored Pomeranians to be sneaked into a mosque
in her oversized handbag. When I was twenty-two, I
chaperoned her in Egypt. At the foot of the Sphinx,
she picked up a handsome, blind music lecturer fifteen
years her junior. They palled around the Mideast
for three weeks while I cooled my heels in cafés,
giving myself headaches from swilling overly
sweet, tooth-decaying mint tea. Perhaps you've
seen a few of her movies. They show up from time
to time on film classics channels on TV. *Kitten
in a Lace Slip, Her Good Name*, and *Shame in Autumn*
were among her big hits. In *A Free Soul*, my favorite,
she plays a slave girl. When a potential buyer tries to pry

open her mouth so he can examine her teeth, she twists

out of his grip, tosses her pretty head, and says, "There is

no path the virtuous cannot tread." Though she has often

ignored me and been oblivious to my needs, though

she is a rotten listener and I have sometimes prayed

for her ruin, when I hear that line, or, rather, when I read it

in flickering, chipped white subtitling (because *A Free Soul*

is among her early silent films), I know my hour has come.

Then love reveals itself to me as all it ever was:

a haphazard mix of charisma, the power of enchanting eyes,

and lies, lies, lies.

On the Fatal Consequences of Going Home with the Wrong Man from the Chicago World's Fair, 1893

Nothing could compare with this bleached dream city, its
    lagoons and gritty
mists, mulberry-paper pavilions, the white temple rising on
    an island
we glimpsed from our gondola's little black cabin. Though
    I'd known him
only fifteen minutes, he quickly kissed off all my lipstick.
    Like many naïve
girls, I mistook fear thudding in my stomach for flutters of
    love. He claimed
to be a doctor, took my wrist to feel my pulse jump. His
    proximity made me
ridiculously dizzy. Arm in arm with the first man to con-
    vince me I was pretty,
we passed the "Guess Your Weight" stand and an alligator
    farm. Aerial acts.
Beer gardens. A gold Buddha calm on his red-lacquered
    throne breathed
not one word of the suffering to come. I saw a wax museum.
    Tigers riding
bicycles. He lured me from the fair at twilight. As I chat-
    tered on, we strolled
a short distance across town to a building of huge rough-
    hewn stones I would

never leave alive. In his gloomy rooms above an apothecary's
    office, I said
I'd seen so many wondrous sights I hardly knew what I
    liked best. The monkey
orchestra. The Ferris wheel. Later, praying did not save me.
    Don't put your
trust in a deep, lulling voice, watery blue eyes, or the
    world's dark mercy.

Mrs. Monster Pens Her Memoirs

Here's a technical question.
Dare I write my fractured past
(squirrelly girlhood, ravenous
adolescence, late-emerging sober
matron graces) in first-person
singular when I'm fragmented
as an undone jigsaw puzzle?
Plural as a litter of kittens?
Always have been—ever since,
well, I can't say "since birth."
No one risked life and limb,
lying on her back in agony,
to squeeze me out of her soupy
womb. My mismatched anatomy's
the sum of chilly-fingered clinicians'
tinkerings: multiple eggs fussed
and fiddled with, desired traits
harvested and recombined.
The resultant goop got fertilized
by the best and brightest bits
pinched from an elite sperm squad
after weeks of stringent auditions.
Thus parentless in any conventional
sense, till a more graceful phrase
unveils itself I'll say "since medical
inception." Since medical inception,

then, my consciousness has been a chorus
full of songs from Broadway plays,
German place names, psalms, recipes,
and the hissing wash of retreating seas.
My recollections (if they be rightly
described as mine) make up a tender
motet hummed by my constituent parts.
I'm a bowl of vertebrate gumbo. But who
among us is not a comically constructed
mutt, a cacophonous anthology?

we are unfashioned creatures,
  but half made up

I remember being kissed on the lip of the Grand Canyon.
Facing that unimaginable geological drop, binoculars
on a black plastic strap round my neck, I read guidebook
entries about coral, mollusks, sea lilies, and fish teeth
trapped in the youngest, uppermost bands of sandstone;
about how the canyon contains roots of an ancient
mountain range. Part of me was tempted to jump,
just in some mindless, "oh here's a tempting cliff edge" way;
to tumble past the Paleozoic, wave at the Precambrian,
salute the Devonian as I plunged by. The vast canyon
so soft with fog no one could see all the way down.

We'd met years earlier
than legend tells it.
At sixteen he fell
out of a tree and
onto me as I walked
underneath
on my way home from school.
Almost broke my arm.
(Some introduction!)
He was a sloppy surgical
collage: his pockmarks,
seams, and scars a shy recital
of his misfortunes. A later model,
I too am patchwork, doctored
hodgepodge, only on invisible,
genetic levels. Ours was a friendship
that slowly *melted into love.*
Never met a more interesting
creature, broken in spirit
though he was.

Returning to the kiss in question, did I imagine
the tickly feel of his beard, his long hair brushing
my shoulder and chin as he leaned into me, his
ragged face lit by something like now-or-neverness?
Surely that happened to "me" and not just some

ghost whose wispy, snipped strands of DNA
I carry around like locks of a dead lover's fair hair.   `
At my age, memory hiccups and tics. But I think
his hands really did shake as we kissed on the canyon
rim, when seconds before I'd been peering studiously
down into the stratified chasm, looking for offshore
islands the guidebook said were embedded
(almost whole) in cakelike layers of limestone.

When I
discovered butter
(thickly buttered everything:
asparagus, sweet rolls, pizza crust, peas;
made triple-decker butter, tomato, and bacon sandwiches—
    all food existed
solely to support copious, built-up strata of butter) and I
    gained 40 lbs, only his
mockery shamed me
into dieting
myself
skinny
again.

He could not accurately be called handsome. Magnetic, yes.
He whispered under his breath constantly, mostly self-critique.
His whirring-buzz-saw aura like a cloud of tiny, irate wasps—
to this I was not immune. His voice was rough. Yet thrumming
beneath his words, a soul-subduing music. He had the temper
of an innovator and martyr, and an intellect, if intensely selfish,
then also wondrously poetic. He liked to bite. He could be
generous (no homeless person passed without his pressing
ten dollars into their hand). After his funeral, I learned he'd
given thousands to my bankrupt dad over the short course
of our marriage, for my monster had known ostracism
and want. His admirer and eulogist, I'm compelled to mention
the jagged beauty of his character: craggy, plummeting, full
of chasms and fossilized burrows—not unlike the Grand Canyon.

(Oh, he had his own crazy notions of
ethics,
conduct,
justice.)

The common appetites of human nature caused him flagrant
        shame.
He never undressed in front of anyone, hated doctors for obvious
reasons, despised the lusts he said twisted his already jerry-rigged
innards. Notions of purity and pollution wracked him. Disgust
        colored

him in. He had to get blind drunk in order to touch me. My
  tickling
gestures of affection were moot. Solemnizing my mind, I re-
  doubled
my resolve to rescue us both (silly, unworldly girl!) by relentless
  devotion,
from hurling through the galaxy in cold, meaningless space; from
  utter
purposelessness. Woman's not man's plaything but his confessor. I
  learned
he could not bear the body, its clumsy functions. "The potter's
  botched
pot," he called it—thought it all seething bacteria and spongy
  fungi.
A filthy, blighted laboratory. Revulsion, disfigurement, and dis-
  trust
heated in the alembic of one destined to be pitifully short-lived.

While you were sleeping, we have remade and improved you.
Thus corrected, you will not recognize yourself on the morrow.

He too liked to stand on the cliff's edge and peer down,
volcanic sediment crunching beneath his heavy boots.
I prayed I might give him some slight ease, and he me.
Yes, *affinity*: we were two of a kind, beasts caged
in awkward human forms. My craving: to be more

formidable—thick legged, with a pulverizing stride.
His longing: to be fully human. Transports of joy
that seized me when I saw a flock of cranes, acacia
trees blooming amidst Milk Lake, or a crocodile
yawning only further affronted him. I wanted him
to stroke my cheek. "Quit looking at me!" he'd snap
when I tried to beam my fond, needy feelings his way.
He refused to be soothed. I wanted him to let me leave
the lights on. Frequently I teased: "Just once I'd like to open
my purse without finding all my lipsticks bitten!" He'd not bathe
for days, eat from the dog's bowl, chain-smoke, lap dirty
water, then want to kiss me. He couldn't help himself.

Beauty only divides the world—
ugliness is far more fascinating,
contains infinitely more variation,
its existence crucial to beauty,
therefore all the more precious.
He used to like to say:
"A crumbling face
such as mine reminds men
what they will ultimately
come to: rot and decay.
And it recalls for them
another unpleasant subject:
history—centuries

of repeated mistakes,
maimings, decimations—
how humans cannot
actually learn or progress
any further (having hit
rock bottom)."

Here are the tips of my ring finger and pinkie.
I would like very much for you to have them.

How real were we to each other?
Opposed, perceiving entities
in private exile,
yet at moments in exquisite balance,
we seemed to know each other's souls.

She believed intellectual companionship the chief, most long-lasting
and happiest aspect of marriage.

All that broken glass strewn on the beach
late one summer night. He wore huge steel-
toed boots of course (never took them off
in anybody's sight—ashamed of his lumpy
misshapen feet, toenails blackened or missing,
perpetually infected, some streaked green
or blue). I was barefoot. A bit tipsy. He

scooped me up and carried me. Giddy,
I thought, I hope he never puts me down.

You don't recover from such sights.
The loved one washed up, drowned,
on the beach. Sand sticking
to his skin like cornmeal. Bodies
burned right there on driftwood pyres at low tide.

(But that was much later.)

In silence
he once brought me gardenias
while I was recovering
from a miscarriage, mistaken
for food poisoning at first,
and an amber necklace
after that time I tried to leave.

Much earlier, at fourteen (two years before I met my monster),
in the pastor's office, on a beanbag chair (incessant crunching
of shifting beans): Rid of it! Free of my burdensome, hideous
virginity! First felt God's friendly intentions then! Could sense
my mind expanding! Uncramped! Ready to receive the world!
Sexual experience for me equaled cause for inebriated relief!
I fervently believe, fellow beings, that we gather strength

by tending and caressing one another, to fend off the long fall,
to steady ourselves against devouring, unending nothingness!
Deflowered by a man of the cloth, and I wasn't even Lutheran!
I wanted to suck up
the essence of men,
mutate, be remade:
become remarkable
and rare—a hybrid,
the best of both sexes,
a reeking genius.

When I looked around I saw and heard of
none like me. Was I, then, a monster,
a blot upon the earth . . . ?

After he drowned
    his flower snapt upon the stalk
a modest procession of lesser
(but nonetheless colorful) lovers
came my way. They too populate
my consciousness, invade me,
take seats, like I'm tiers of parade-ground
bleachers (half-empty due to faint rain).
But a respectable crowd gathers,
whistles and cheers as the solemn
founders of this small town,

sheltering under umbrellas,

march to the accompaniment

of a brass band. They file by,

these former lovers of mine,

some waving painted banners:

HI! I'M THE ONE WHOSE POSTCOITAL SWEAT SMELLED
   LIKE CELERY!

                                        (And so on.)

After all this time, I get some of them mixed up.

In my mind, they become composite—they fuse,

seeming to have the front end

of one animal and the rear of another.

Then they all begin marching

        in separate

                directions

                                        till they grow so small I can hardly see them anymore.

Monster Roll Call:

Great-horned turtle

Hundred-handed giant

Ogres who capsize boats

    and devour the occupants

"Ever-chomping" azure dragon

creature brought from Egypt to Rome

preserved in honey

"Monsters who sit beside their victims'

Lopped-off heads and weep"

Hag with a deadly stare

Serpent with the face of a woman

Bog monster

Two huge carnivorous birds, who unceasingly

call to one another

A cobbled-together freakish being

with "a heart that scorns disguise"

Cerberus the three-headed dog

(who'd been hit

by a car and ever after limped,

her noses like three Greek olives,

three different earsplitting barks;

the soul

of devotion, that dear brave

dog, and not a monster at all)

"I do not believe you are what you seem to be."

What lies behind that black-lipped visage?

If only someone else could slip inside this body

(the soul's meaty Halloween costume:

sometimes it's pinkish, or the brackish color of wet wood:

depends on my mood) and look out through these pinhole eyes,
work the opposable thumb, squeeze into the driver's seat
beside me, they could pilot this rig awhile while I sleep.
I am so tired. And I demand to know:
who stuffed me into this old-lady suit and how
do I burst out now—unzip it and step free?

I only wished to be necessary to him. You see,
tenderness frightened him more than violence.
Yes, tenderness with its sappy, jam-sweet stickiness,
its incriminating stains. Thus temporarily our tattered
souls get mended with thin, slobbery, homemade glue.
And will the besmirched soul be licked clean
by shame's rough, motherly tongue? Can you at last
understand my feelings? A long and difficult voyage
ahead, friendless, without him now. *Seas will not divide us*
(he promised!), *or years elapse before we see one another again.*
But he washed ashore days later, with kelp in his hair.

Make him love me.
This was my conquest,
my mantra.
I donned armor,
ready to do battle.
And do not believe,
dear reader, that I

carried no sword.
For there are
male spirits,
confined by mistake
in female frames,
and I believe
I have been
such a one.

IV.

Elegy

the room did not lurch

when he was all the priest you needed
perched next to your bed the last five
days of your life as purple wisteria dripped
from the arbor you'd built right outside
last year climbing the handyman's ladder
a bit weak yet still able to savor actions
rationed perhaps performed for the last
time you toiled in weathered yellow leather
gardening gloves pruning while being uprooted
change of venue approaching your body's
valise tied shut with frayed twine now
your clothes have been given away bedding
laundered room aired molecules of your blue
sense of humor loosed into fickle April haze
like microscopic weather balloons to whom
did you leave your false eyelashes your work
ethic your taste for the stick-to-the-ribs foods
of your youth an abject gooseneck lamp
on your nightstand hangs its head and prays
the way mute objects do when left behind
strange it doesn't implode make some move
to accompany you but rather remains like
the bust of some shamed alien conqueror
its long neck bent like a penitent swan's

Elegy with Peonies

Peonies may indeed be the sluttiest
flowers. Sunk in their ruffles, high on
their own old-rose perfume, they're

all voluptuous appetite. Heavy-headed
billowy blooms in botanical drag,
they make showy hibiscus and

thick-pistilled lilies look like wallpaper
motifs from a more uptight era.
Peonies' lives are exceedingly brief.

The tawdry blossoms babble drunkenly
to passing bees in midsummer till they lose
their splendid crowns, which lie

shattered on wet, trampled grass. Queen
Anne's lace stands by smug, correct,
the picture of decorum. Dear Ed, intemperate

old friend, a phone call this morning
brings me news of your suicide. Angry note
stuffed in your pocket after you'd gulped

your overprescribed meds all at once, you
collapsed wending your way up to the roof.
I wept, remembering how you sometimes liked

to wear skirts, and how handsome you looked
in them—*Braveheart* meets Catholic schoolgirl.
Could your brilliance and beauty ever be prized

from the fact that you were always agonized,
always drowning? I hope the heaven you're in
is replete with heavy metal riffs, science quizzes,

bisexual angels, endless wildness of mind,
and fields of eternally peaking peonies.

Dig

I dig most those covert parts of a song
that are hardly song at all, when the singer
sucks in a trembly breath to fuel her next lyric.
That frayed inhalation the microphone picks up,
that amplified fragment of animal gasp

is what gets me: precursor to all creaturely music.
When we first kissed, the boy took a deep,
chest-filling breath, as though preparing to dive
for treasure nestled on some river bottom. Later
we dug up his ancestors' graves, in the name

of archaeology—unearthed encrusted medallions
and baskets. We excavated a crumbling
staircase with ass-polished banisters, chipped
sediment from a stone effigy of an infant prince
cupping his penis as he sleeps. We unsealed

caves containing stoppered jars labeled "transcendent
experiences," "senseless bickering," "other forms of con-
    sciousness,"
"the voice of exceptions," and "what we'll miss most."
    When he
tripped over an ornamented chest with "unclassified
residuum" written in ancient script on the lid, damaging

it badly, he was suitably chagrined. "The style
of an apology should be simple and brief," he stammered,
all distraught, sure I was going to sack him. Black
goats wandered the valley below. As he yammered on,
I inventoried the tools and maps in my backpack, tried

to look stern and not laugh, emptied my sandals.
This boy returned tenfold any affection he was given;
his earnest, besmirched face as calming to me
as the word "libation." My roaring inner wish
was to dunk his fingers in strong coffee and nibble

them like buttermilk crullers back home. If I'd had
any sense I would have said so in his guttural native tongue.
If I've told you once I've told you a thousand times, it's bad form
to be jealous of the dead. Never your rival, he was simply a boy
who was hard on his toys, myself chief among them.

Broken Lines

It's difficult, though, not to feel
left behind by your suicide,
like a child who flunked
third grade plunked down
in a rickety folding chair
to watch a parade of classmates
graduate. The earth still pirouettes.
Horse doctors continue to write
haiku and mend split hooves.
We keep telling each other
you had the right (since every-
body does) and made a brave end.
But how're we supposed to maintain
after you so brutally subtracted yourself
from the habitable? Our anguish
areas are ever expanding, just like our
horizons. Keep an eye on us, will ya?
Don't let your friends get too sullen
or puckered. Deep in the background
of erudite or wasted conversations,
let us intuit you as subtext,
as static, some fuzzy transmission
from the deserted cities you've got
all to yourself now, big guy.

Dear Departed,

Five ice-glazed trees keeled over
today. Did that racket disturb your
permanent faint? Sorry our pale
ministrations failed. Does mud hold
grudges? Don't overthink your response,
once-upright, diffident citizen. May we
address you directly? Can you tell if
you're open or closed? Did God uncork
your mouth, roll a boulder from your
yawn? What's the moment of rising like?
Did earth melt you down and chug you
like fortified wine? Thought or said,
your name sparks painful cravings lately:
to lick your pearl cuff links or singe
one's fingers on that scalp-sized brush-
fire formerly known as your hair. One
careless doctor cannot sunder us, buddy.
Tomorrow's existence feels borrowed,
or bought with your dregs. Dumb as your
exit struck us, we bask in every mention
of your dispersed, weedy-meadow
self, perfected friend gone elemental.

Dusk

Dear, I can't subsist on this diet
(really more of a fast—celery
seed and a soft word every other
month) any longer. Is that blood
on your pillowcase or another girl's
lipstick? I want you to know,
I've had such unalloyed joy
over the past several decades,
smelling your hair and petting
your sweat-beaded feet while
you were asleep. It was far sweeter
than I ever thought possible.
But my ancestors are welling up
in me now and keep nudging me
toward the door. Bells are rung,
harps are played: recessional music.
We both know the theater will close
in a few minutes. If you had been
more attentive or a better pretender,
I could have run on fumes for a few
more years, sipping snowmelt,
remaining quite high on it. Let
the record show, I recited prayers

for your perpetual ascension
and good health as I laid this note
in its frozen envelope on your desk
and left, taking both dogs, the teal
parakeet, and the black cat with me.
They got custody of our love.

Midlife Lullaby

Fear not the tarnish and diminishments of age
or its insane revelations as you creak, leak, and freak
your way to the grave. Never relinquish ties
to exiles, to juiced-up boozers and the bamboozled.
Like you, they're solid citizens anguish nearly polished
off (but not yet!), burnished veterans gilded by loss,
who glint like old bowling trophies in the right light.
"Extinguishment is still far away," we repeat under
our breaths at bedtime, like children who can't
remember their prayers. Come morning we'll step
out for a meatloaf sandwich (one our grown son
dubbed "meat-load" sandwich back when he was a ticklish
kid squishing it flat with his little hand so it'd fit into
his mouth.) A humble dish with radish garnish,
it gives sagging spirits a lift and beguiles our tongues
with onions, mustard, and mortal sweetness welling
up from deep in the beef, which, if meat could speak
might moo or sigh: "Yes, I too was well fed in my time."

Dedications

Moon Salutation (p. 19) is for Elaine Equi.

Advice from a Caterpillar (p. 23) is for Dinah Lenney.

Moths (p. 24) is for Bernard Cooper.

Interview with a Dog (p. 33) is for Chris Green.

Chant of the Hallucinogenic Plants (p. 35) is
    for Francesca Gabbiani.

At the Back of a Closet, Two Dresses Converse (p. 39) is
    for David Trinidad.

How to Wear Hats (p. 41) is for Sean Heaney.

The Chamber of Maiden Thought (p. 42) is
    for Dorna Khazeni.

Untranslatable (p. 46) is for David Lehman.

During a Wet Spring, Long Ago (p. 48) is in memory
    of Judith Moore.

Mrs. Monster Pens Her Memoirs (p. 55) is
    for Lyndall Gordon.

the room did not lurch (p. 71) is in memory
    of Brian Miller.

Elegy with Peonies (p. 72) is in memory of
    Edward Young Smith.

Broken Lines (p. 76) is in memory of Liam Rector.

About the Author

Amy Gerstler is a writer of poetry, nonfiction, and journalism who lives in Los Angeles. Her previous eleven books include *Medicine*, *Crown of Weeds*, which won a California Book Award, *Nerve Storm*, and *Bitter Angel*, which won the National Book Critics Circle Award. Her poems have appeared in a variety of magazines and anthologies, including *The New Yorker*, *The Paris Review*, *American Poetry Review*, and several volumes of *Best American Poetry* and *The Norton Anthology of Postmodern America Poetry*, and her journalism and art criticism have appeared in *Artforum*, *The Village Voice*, *Los Angeles Magazine*, *Los Angeles Times*, *Art and Antiques*, and numerous other publications. She teaches in the graduate fine arts department at Art Center, College of Design, in Pasadena, California. She is a member of the core faculty of the Bennington Writing Seminars MFA program at Bennington College in Vermont, and teaches at the University of Southern California in the MPW program. She has taught writing and/or art at the California Institute of the Arts, Cal Tech, the University of California at Irvine, the University of Utah, and elsewhere.

JOHN ASHBERY
Selected Poems
Self-Portrait in a Convex
Mirror

TED BERRIGAN
The Sonnets

JOE BONOMO
Installations

PHILIP BOOTH
Selves

JIM CARROLL
Fear of Dreaming:
The Selected Poems
Living at the Movies
Void of Course

ALISON HAWTHORNE
DEMING
Genius Loci
Rope

CARL DENNIS
New and Selected Poems
1974-2004
Practical Gods
Ranking the Wishes
Unknown Friends

DIANE DI PRIMA
Loba

STUART DISCHELL
Backwards Days
Dig Safe

STEPHEN DOBYNS
Velocities: New and
Selected Poems,
1966–1992

EDWARD DORN
Way More West: New
and Selected Poems

AMY GERSTLER
Crown of Weeds: Poems
Dearest Creature
Ghost Girl
Medicine
Nerve Storm

EUGENE GLORIA
Drivers at the Short-Time
Motel
Hoodlum Birds

DEBORA GREGER
Desert Fathers, Uranium
Daughters
God
Men, Women, and Ghosts
Western Art

TERRANCE HAYES
Hip Logic
Wind in a Box

ROBERT HUNTER
Sentinel and Other Poems

MARY KARR
Viper Rum

WILLIAM KECKLER
Sanskrit of the Body

JACK KEROUAC
Book of Sketches
Book of Blues
Book of Haikus

JOANNA KLINK
Circadian

JOANNE KYGER
As Ever: Selected Poems

ANN LAUTERBACH
Hum
If In Time:
Selected Poems,
1975–2000
On a Stair
Or to Begin Again

CORINNE LEE
PYX

PHILLIS LEVIN
May Day
Mercury

WILLIAM LOGAN
Macbeth in Venice
Strange Flesh
The Whispering Gallery

ADRIAN MATEJKA
Mixology

MICHAEL MCCLURE
Huge Dreams: San Francisco
and Beat Poems

DAVID MELTZER
David's Copy:
The Selected Poems of
David Meltzer

CAROL MUSKE
An Octave above Thunder
Red Trousseau

ALICE NOTLEY
The Descent of Alette
Disobedience
In the Pines
Mysteries of Small Houses

LAWRENCE RAAB
The History of Forgetting
Visible Signs: New and
Selected Poems

BARBARA RAS
One Hidden Stuff

PATTIANN ROGERS
Generations
Wayfare

WILLIAM STOBB
Nervous Systems

TRYFON TOLIDES
An Almost Pure Empty
Walking

ANNE WALDMAN
Kill or Cure
Manatee/Humanity
Structure of the World
Compared to a Bubble

JAMES WELCH
Riding the Earthboy 40

PHILIP WHALEN
Overtime: Selected Poems

ROBERT WRIGLEY
Earthly Meditations:
New and Selected Poems
Lives of the Animals
Reign of Snakes

MARK YAKICH
The Importance of Peeling
Potatoes in Ukraine
Unrelated Individuals
Forming a Group
Waiting to Cross

JOHN YAU
Borrowed Love Poems
Paradiso Diaspora